☞ See List of Plays on 2d, 3d and 4th pages of Cover.

No. CXLV.

THE MINOR DRAMA.

COLUMBUS

EL FILIBUSTERO!!

A New and audaciously Original

HISTRICO-PLAGARISTIC, ANTE-NATIONAL, PRE-PATRIOTIC,

AND COMIC CONFUSION OF CIRCUMSTANCES,

RUNNING THROUGH

TWO ACTS AND FOUR CENTURIES!

BY JOHN BROUGHAM, COMEDIAN.

AS PERFORMED AT BURTON THRATRE, DECEMBER, 1857.
AND AT HOLIDAY STREET THEATRE, BALTIMORE, 1858.

NEW-YORK:
SAMUEL FRENCH,
122 NASSAU STREET, (UP STAIRS.)

PRICE,] [12½ CENTS.

FRENCH'S STANDARD DRAMA,

Price 12½ Cents each.– Bound Volumes $1.

VOL. I.

1. Ion,
2. Fazio,
3. The Lady of Lyons,
4. Richelieu,
5. The Wife,
6. The Honeymoon,
7. The School for Scandal
8. Money,

With a Portrait and Memoir of Mrs. A. C. MOWATT.

VOL. II.

9. The Stranger,
10. Grandfather White-
11. Richard III. [head,
12. Love's Sacrifice,
13. The Gamester, [ache,
14. A Cure for the Heart-
15. The Hunchback,
16. Don Cæsar de Bazan,

With a Portrait and Memoir of Mr. CHARLES KEAN.

VOL. III.

17. The Poor Gentleman,
18. Hamlet,
19. Charles II.
20. Venice Preserved,
21. Pizarro,
22. The Love Chase,
23. Othello, [lings,
24. Lend me Five Shil-

With a Portrait and Memoir of Mr. W. E. BURTON.

VOL. IV.

25. Virginius,
26. King of the Commons
27. London Assurance,
28. The Rent Day,
29. Two Gentlemen of Verona,
30. The Jealous Wife,
31. The Rivals,
32. Perfection,

With a Portrait and Memoir of J. H. HACKETT

VOL. V.

33. A New Way to Pay Old Debts,
34. Look Before You Leap
35. King John,
36. Nervous Man,
37. Damon and Pythias,
38. Clandestine Marriage
39. William Tell,
40. Day after the Wedding

With a Portrait and Memoir of G. COLMAN, the Elder.

VOL. VI.

41. Speed the Plough,
42. Romeo and Juliet,
43. Feudal Times,
44. Charles the Twelfth,
45. The Bridal,
46. The Follies of a Night
47. The Iron Chest,
48. Faint Heart Never Won Fair Lady,

With a Portrait and Memoir of E. BULWER LYTTON.

VOL. VII.

49. Road to Ruin,
50. Macbeth,
51. Temper,
52. Evadne,
53. Bertram,
54. The Duenna,
55. Much Ado About Nothing,
56. The Critic,

With a Portrait and Memoir of R. B. SHERIDAN.

VOL. VIII.

57. The Apostate,
58. Twelfth Night,
59 Brutus,
60. Simpson & Co.
61. Merchant of Venice,
62. Old Heads and Young Hearts,
63. Mountaineers.
64. Three Weeks After Marriage.

With a Portrait and Memoir of Mr. GEORGE H. BARRETT.

VOL. IX.

65. Love,
66. As You Like It,
67. The Elder Brother,
68. Werner,
69. Gisippus,
70. Town and Country.
71. King Lear,
72. Blue Devils,

With a Portrait and Memoir of Mrs. SHAW.

VOL. X.

73. Henry VIII.
74. Married and Single,
75. Henry IV.
76. Paul Pry.
77. Guy Mannering,
78. Sweethearts and Wives,
79. Serious Family.
80. She Stoops to Conquer,

With a Portrait and Memoir of Miss C. CUSHMAN.

VOL. XI.

81. Julius Cæsar,
82. Vicar of Wakefield,
83. Leap Year,
84. The Catspaw,
85. The Passing Cloud,
86. Drunkard,
87. Rob Roy,
88. George Barnwell,

With a Portrait and Memoir of Mrs. JOHN SEFTON.

VOL. XII.

89. Ingomar,
90. Sketches in India,
91. Two Friends,
92. Jane Shore,
93. Corsican Brothers,
94. Mind Your Own Business,
95. Writing on the Wall,
96. Heir at Law,

With a Portrait and Memoir of Mr. THOMAS HAMBLIN.

VOL. XIII.

97. Soldier's Daughter,
98. Douglas,
99. Marco Spada,
100. Nature's Nobleman,
101. Sardanapalus,
102. Civilization,
103. The Robbers,
104. Katharine and Petruchio.

With a Portrait and Memoir of Mr. EDWIN FOREST.

VOL. XIV.

105. Game of Love,
106. Midsummer Night's Dream,
107. Ernestine,
108. Rag Picker of Paris,
109. Flying Dutchman,
110. Hypocrite,
111. Therese,
112. La Tour de Nesle,

With a Portrait and Memoir of Mr. JOHN BROUGHAM.

VOL. XV.

113. Ireland As It Is,
114. Sea of Ice.
115. Seven Clerks,
116. Game of Life,
117. Forty Thieves,
118. Bryan Boroihme,
119. Romance & Reality.
120. Ugolino,

With a Portrait and Memoir of Mr. BARNEY WILLIAMS.

VOL. XVI.

121. The Tempest,
122. The Pilot,
123. Carpenter of Rouen,
124. King's Rival,
125. Little Treasure,
126. Dombey and Son,
127. Parents and Guard-
128. Jewess. [ians,

VOL. XVII.

129. Camille,
130. Married Life,
131. Wenlock of Wenlock
132. Rose of Ettrickvale,
133. David Copperfield,
134. Aline, or the Rose of
135. Pauline, [Killarney,
136. Jane Eyre.

VOL. XVIII.

137. Night and Morning,
138. Æthiop,
139. Three Guardsmen,
140. Tom Cringle, [ken.
141. Henriette, the Forsa-
142. Eustache Baudin,
143. Ernest Maltravers,
144. Bold Dragoons.

VOL. XIX.

145. Dred, or the Dismal Swamp,
146. Last Days of Pom-
147. Esmeralda, [peii,
148. Peter Wilkins,
149. Ben the Boatswain,
150. Jonathan Bradford,
151. Retribution,
152. Minerali.

VOL. XX.

153. French Spy,
154. Wept of Wish-ton Wish,
155. Evil Genius,
156. Ben Bolt,
157. Sailor of France,
158. Red Mask,
159. Life of an Actress,
160. Wedding Day.

VOL. XXI.

161. All's Fair in Love,
162. Hofer,
163. Self,
164. Cinderella,
165. Phantom,
166. Franklin,
167. The Gunmaker of Moscow,
168. The Love of a Prince

VOL. XXII.

169. Son of the Night,
170. Rory O'More,
171. Golden Eagle,
172. Rienzi.
173. Broken Sword,
174. Rip Van Winkle,
175. Isabelle.
176. Heart of Midlothian.

VOL. XXIII.

177. Actress of Padua,
178. Floating Beacon,
179. Bride of Lammermoor, [ges,
180. Cataract of the Gan-
181. Robber of the Rhine
182. School of Reform,
183. Wandering Boys,
184. Mazeppa.

VOL. XXIV.

185. Young New York.
186. The Victims.
187 Romance after Mar-
188 Brigand, [riage,
189 Poor of New York,
190 Ambrose Gwinett,
191 Raymond and Agnes,
192 Gambler's Fate,

[*Catalogue continued on third page of cover.*]

THE MINOR DRAMA.

The Acting Edition.

No. CXLV.

COLUMBUS

EL FILIBUSTERO!!

A NEW AND AUDACIOUSLY ORIGINAL HISTORICO-PLAGIARISTIC, ANTE-NATIONAL, PRE-PATRIOTIC, AND OMNI-LOCAL CONFUSION OF CIRCUMSTANCES, RUNNING THROUGH

TWO ACTS AND FOUR CENTURIES.

BY JOHN BROUGHAM, COMEDIAN.

AS PERFORMED AT BURTON'S THEATRE, DECEMBER, 1857
AND AT HOLLIDAY STREET THEATRE, BALTIMORE, 1858.

NEW YORK:
SAMUEL FRENCH,
122 NASSAU STREET, (UP STAIRS.)

DISTRIBUTION OF CHARACTERS,

GOOD, BAD AND INDIFFERENT.

Character	Actor
FERDINAND, King of Arragon—an aggressive and progressive monarch, of rather a speculative turn, with a good many irons on the fire, besides an eye on Castile, - - - -	Mr. Mark Smith.
JUAN RODERIGUES DE FONSECA, Archdeacon of Seville, keeper of the king's conscience, [a handsome sinecure,] and court spiritual adviser generally, therefore, naturally opposed to Columbus and the spread of knowledge, - -	Mr. Holman.
FERNANDO DE TALAVERA, an old picture, very much improved by time, - - -	Mr. Barrett.
LUIS DE ST. ANGEL, a contented office-holder, pursuing the even tenor of his way, - -	Mr. Alleyne.
ALONZO DE QUINTANELLA, a courtier of much lower note, - . - - - -	Mr. Gledhill.
DON CHRISTOVAL COLON alias COLUMBUS, a clairvoyant voyager, whose filibustering expedition gave rise at the time to a world of speculation,	Mr. Brougham.
DIEGO, a semicolon among the king's pages, -	Miss Orten.

Character	Description	Actor
VASCO NUNEZ,	Distinguished members of the Historical Society, now meeting together for the first time.	Mr. Hurley.
HERNANDO CORTEZ,		Mr. Atkins.
AMERIGO VESPUCCI,		Mr. Paul.
PONCE DE LEON,		Mr. Lawson.
SANCHO RUIS,	A noisy crew of mutinous Seapoys.	Mr. McRae.
PEDRO NINO,		Mr. Bishop.
BARTOLOMEO,		Mr. Hayes.
JUAN PEREZ,		Mr. Bruce.
&c., &c.		

Character	Actor
ISABELLA, wife of Ferdinand, possessor of half-a-crown by marriage rite, and a whole one by right of having to carry its weight on her own shoulders,	Mrs. Holman.
COLUMBIA, a national debutante, her first appearance on any stage, - - -	Mrs. L. W. Davenport.
LITTLE MISS KANSAS, a discordant element,	Miss Taylor.

Members of Reception Committee, Aldermen, Discontented Politicians, Independent Voters, and other natural curiosities by Competent Representatives.

Full-grown States, Juvenile Territories, &c., by an Energetic Host of Auxiliaries.

COLUMBUS.

ACT I.

SCENE I.—*Hall of Audience in King Ferdinand's Palace.*

KING, QUEEN, *and an entire pack of court cards, discovered.*

COMPLIMENTARY CHORUS, ["*Gustavus,*"] *by the courtiers, enthusiastic and ecomiastic, as in duty bound.*

Hail! oh, king of Arragon!
Reign! oh, princely paragon!
Down upon your marrowbone,
Long live the king!
Monarch mightier is he, sir,
Than Joe Smith or Julius Cæsar,
Brigham Young or Nebuchudnezzar,
Long live the king!
And hail to Isabella, too,
For she's a right good fellow, too,
And a right good tune to bellow to,
Is long live the queen!
She's fairer than the fairest fairy,
Sweeter than the Scottish Mary,
Nymph or Nereiad there's n'ary
One like our queen.
[*Cheers from the administration.*

King. This cheering fire, defenders of the great,
Is grateful to our royal tympanum, of late
Elated by our victories among
Those mongrel Moors, to hear our praises sung
We've had no time; but now the wars are ended,
And in the usual way, our faith defended,
That is by slaying every slavish minion
Who dares to differ with us in opinion.

Although by proxy those great deeds were done,
We think we've earned the right to have some fun;
So loud let every office-holder shout,
Or else we'll send them to the right about.
[*The several sticks shout accordingly.*
Louder, you puddin' heads, aldermen and all,
Or else our city hall we'll overhaul,
And cut your heavy jobs and contracts down,
And then we'll see who'll represent the town.
Tell us what news is stirring in the city?

Fonseca. So please you, sire, the Vigilance Committee
A foolish foreigner this day has found,
Who swears, confound him, that the world is round,
And swings, on what the fellow calls its *axis*,
Just once a year.

King. He's thinking of the taxes.

Fonseca. It taxes both credulity and patience
To listen to the mountebank's relations.

Queen. Perhaps he's right—let's ask him here to sup,
There may be something in——

King. My love, shut up.

Fonseca. But that's not all he says.

King. I want to know.
What does he say?

Fonseca. He says, my liege, below
There is a corresponding half-world——

King. We know better
For did it correspond we'd have a letter.
We've nothing from that latitude, in fine
We hav'n't had an equinoctial line—
So it's all bosh.

Queen. 'Twould be as well to hear
The man himself.

King. Now, don't you interfere.

Fonseca. And more than this—your majesty will laugh,
Of course—the fool asserts, the other half
Has mountains, vallies, seas, just like our own;
With men and women——

King. What, turned upside down!
Strange kind of man, to think mankind, like flies,
Could in such strange position stand—he lies.

Fonseca. But, above all, the chap maintains that gold
And precious gems lie there in heaps untold.

Queen. What, diamonds?

Fonseca. And pearls of countless price,
Rubies and amethysts.

Queen. Take my advice
And look into this matter.

King. You look out;
Bell, hold your tongue—we know what we're about.

Let some one summon here this foreign catiff
Who thus presumes to know more than a native.
Hast heard his name?

Fernando de Talevera. Columbus.

King. That's a dove.

Queen. I like it—'tis the type of peace and love—
You called me so at first.

King. Be quiet, do;
Don't talk, my dove, until you head your *coo.*
Who is this pigeon?

Fernando. I saw him hawking
Some maps and charts; sad and fatigued with walking,
He rested on a convent step—his son
Lay near him, hunger-pinched and wan
With weakness—yet the heartless crowd passed on,
Even without the tribute of a sigh.
At length, a poor friar, himself not overfed,
Gave to the wanderers a loaf of bread.
The gift was timely, yet the proud man's soul,
I plainly saw, revolted at the dole,
Although 'twas thankfully received. He woke
The famine-stricken boy, and quickly broke
The loaf in two—one half the lad received,
And with such ravenous haste—it deeper grieved
The sorrowing man. I read his anxious fears;
I saw the dry crust moistened with his tears,
And turned away dimsighted and heart-sick.

King. I'll take my oath that friar was a brick.
He's poor, it seems, despite of all his pains—
Then, ten to one, the fellow's cursed with brains.
If so, I'll steal 'em, for mere brains *alone* are
Seldom any use to the first owner.
[*Laughing heard without*

CHORUS. [*Outside.*]

Laughing Chorus, "Der Freischutz."

Such madman's words, how shall we style 'em?
The ass has broke from some asylum;
A world across the western sea!
'Twon't do, Columbus—no, siree.

Ecco Italiani, "Trovatore."

Scizzerrere!
Oh fel magia mosbio
As a marchera, che si won't returno,
Scizzerere!
Ti himup to some trio,
Predo, for here he cant Soggiurno!

Columbus. [*Without.*]

Bi guingo, lam orti the crowdo,
Astar, nota onei se nir.
Ah mi tiseri—
Ah mi tiseri Mustay.
Hadio hadio buta dimo
To geta Sangarie.

Chorus.

Du tell, du tel guist erim
The luni supposès notin.
Scizzerere!
De te nim ti Sonli ad ute uno.

Columbus.

De te nim O damit, de te nim O no.

King. Go, bring him in—and now we'll pump him dryer
Than the dry crust he got from that same friar.
Queen. Unworthy thought.
King. Bell, if there's any tin,
You'll tintinnabulate—I mean ring in.
If there's a chance, the main one you won't lose,
But caution and precaution both we'll use.
We'll see this mariner—if aught accrues
From his projected cruise, we won't reject it,
But with the glory of our reign connect it.
By our own royal judgment we'll abide,
And if we find him slippery, let him slide.
Fonseca. I hope your majesty will deign to pause.
Before this man, who scouts our mundane laws,
You thus encourage—our estate it shocks
That he should trifle with the orthodox.
The church has settled that the world is flat.
King. There cannot be the slightest doubt of that.
He comes—don't fear, we'll find out his intents.

Enter COLUMBUS, *peddling stationery.*

Col. Twenty-five maps of the world for four cents.
King. Who are you, stranger, that with daring speech
A new cosmogany presume to teach?
Col. A ci-devant poor flat-boat captain, sire.
King. Flat broke 'twould seem to judge from your attire.
Go on, unfold yourself, pay out.
Col. My lord, I will.
Will you oblige me with the chord? [*To leader*

Biographic Cantata.

Introductory Recitative.

Mio simplissima storio dost thou requesto,
Oh give caro unto mi relazioni,
But if this foreign lingo, you cannot digesto
I'll try the purissimo Anglo Saxoni.

Aria Familiaria.

My name it is Columbus, I was born in Genoa
Of poor but honest parents, so the story always goes.
My father was a mariner, and he mar-ri-ed my mother there,
And I was the offspring as you may readily suppose.
Sweet infancy's days when the brain very little *wit* is in,
As is mostly the case passed unconciously bye,
Oh my parent's expected I'd become a steady sober citizen,
But I was bound to be a sailor boy, by jingo, or die.

For many a long year I have plough'd the wild ocean,
And many strange notians and natives have seen,
But now in my head I have got a sort of notion
That there's some place else somewhere that aint been seen yet.
To find this place out is the only thing I live for,
Ambition and fame in that single path lie
Just to help me along some assistance pray give, for
I'm bound to find Columbia, by jingo, or die!

King. What is't youv'e got within your silly brain?
Col. A Main land, sire, there is beyond the Main.
Fonseca. Let it remain there.
King. Stop a minute—
We'll hear him talk, there may be something in it.
Queen. Pearls and rubies grow there, we are told?—
King. Now do be quiet;—aye, and lots of gold.
Col. I'm almost weary, sire, of telling o'er
To Princes all the gifts I have in store,
For him who will accept the golden key,
And will for such a chance my patron be.
To my own land I fain would give the prize,
But there was no speculation in their eyes,
And not a real but to realise
My ardent Spirit's hope's, would they advance,
French leave I took of them, and unto France
Laden with gall, pursued my weary way,
But the great Lewis had by reckless play
Collapsed his treasury, for like a stoker
The British King had singed him at drawpoker,
The winning King I tried, while he was flush,
But for my suit he did'nt care a rush,

Now sad and broken down, I've wandered here,
Without one ray my onward path to cheer—
The street my lodging and the stones my bed,
An airy lodging for I've 'nary red!

Fonseca. Audacious peddler! what is this we hear—
You say our World is but a hemisphere,
And there's another somewhere under ground
That joined with it goes alway's bobbing round.

Col. This earth's a globe.

King. Well, that's a round assertion—
Then tell us, if you please, just for diversion,
What does it rest on?

Col. Circumambient space—

King. Circum-fiddlesticks—you *are* a case!
And what's the reason that it doesn't drop?

Col. In endless revolution like a top
It sleeps,—thus exquisitely poised in air
By equalized attraction.

Tonseca. Fool—beware!
We canot listen to such words as these,
The stake has blazed for lighter heresies!

King. A lunatic—there's not a doubt of that—
But in the meal-tub there *may* be a cat.

Queen. Poor man! We must do something for him.

King. Stay!
Wait 'till we find out if the thing will pay,
Friend Christopher, we're sorry for your plight,
But pledge our royal word to make it right
If to our realm you'll add some foreign nation,
Rich and disposed to stand extreme taxation,
Prove you can do this, so that none can doubt it,
And we shall give you—leave to set about.

Col. But, sire, my scheme needs money.

King. Well, then *share* it—
Get up a joint stock and don't over-"*bear*" it.

Col. Craft I must have to sail in.

King. "Quantum suf."
Once you're in Wall street, you'll find craft enough,
You dreamy fellow's, that don't know the ropes
Sit down and starve upon your empty hopes,
While sharper dunces thrive.

Col. I fain would know
The way.

King. To raise the wind you'll have to "blow,"
We'll call our company—" the *Anti-Panic*
Perpetual Gold Producing Oceanic,"
And true *de facto* high old "Life and Trust—"
Bound in due time to spread itself—

Col. And bust.

King. Of course, but not till we go in and win,

Capital we'll call five millions to begin.
Col. I shall not need a third.
King. Oh! have no fears,—
We must provide for fast clerks and cashiers,
Armies of "Blowers"—"Runners" and "Advisers"—
"Committees"—"Lobbyers" and "Advertisers"—
And for your president a small gratuity.
Some thirty thousand would'nt hurt us.
Col. Query!
King. You would'nt go below our friends in Erie—
Col. My aspirations, sire, you only mock
Who would be fools enough to take such stock:
King. Who, Sir?—Why everybody! what stupidity,
If you but nicely tickle their cupidity!
I'll prove it in an instant. Ho! a Court!
[*The court makes an immediate advance*
My lords, we're going to make you a report
Of the first meeting for consolidation,
Of our new filibustering association,—
I mean for the encouragement of emigration,—
Present—the president, myself—ahem!
Secretary and Treasurer *pro tem*—
Profits enormous, and the outlay small.
Col. An old man's wearied life, perhaps, that's all.
King. Who'll venture while the wheel of fortune whirls,
Dividend's paid in gold or Jersey pearls:
You should'nt let a chance like this go bye.
Ferdinand. I'll take some stock!
Courtiers. And I—and I—&c.
Fonseca. Just put me down.
King. Archbishop, you a byer?
Fonseca Prudence is a cardinal virtue, sire.
King. Now we must try the street—Pope say's you know,
Man wants but [*Jacob*] little here below—
And we're all right.
Col. Then care and sorrow's past,
Hope dawns and life's worth living for at last!
[*Flings away maps and stands abstracted.*
Fonseca. Look at the peddler!
King. Just as sure as fate
He's in a beautiful clairvoyant state!
Columbus! Why are you in such amaze?
Col. Time onward passes, and my mental gaze
Is on the future, lo! I see a land
Where nature seems to frame with practised hand
Her last most wonderous work! before me rise
Mountains of solid rock that rift the skies,—
Imperial vallies with rich verdure crowned
For leagues illimitable smile around,
While through them subject seas for rivers run

From ice bonnd tracts to where the tropic sun
Breeds in the teeming ooze strange monstrous things—
I see upswelling from exhaustless springs,
Great lakes appear upon whose surface wide
The banded navies of the earth may ride,
I see tremendous cataract's emerge
From cloud aspiring heights, whose slippery verge
Tremendous ocean's momently roll o'er,
Assaulting with unmitigated roar
The stunned and shattered ear of trembling day
That wounded, weeps in glistening tears of spray!

King. We grieve your sensibility to shock,
See something else or down will go our stock.

Col. I see upspringing from the fruitful breast
Of the beneficent and boundless West,
Uncounted acres of life-giving grain,
Wave o'er the gently undulating plain,
So tall each blade that you can scarcely touch
The top!

King. Ah! now, my blade, you see too much.

Col. Within the limits of the southern zone
I see plantations, thickly overgrown
With a small shrub in whose white flower lies
A revenue of millions!

King. You surprise
Us now, we'll cotton to that tree!
Go on, old fellow, what else do you see?

Col. Some withered weeds—

King. Pooh!

Col. From which men can evoke
Profit as wonderful!

King. From what?

Col. From smoke.

King. Ah, now you're in the clouds again. Good gracious!
Think of the stock, and don't be so fugacious.

Col. I see a river, through whose limpid stream,
Pastolus like, the yellow pebbles gleam;
Flowing through regions, where great heaps of gold,
Uncared for, lie in affluence untold,
Thick as autumnal leaves, the precious store.

King. My eyes! why didn't you see that before?
We'll go ourself, we mean we shall "go in."
Go on.

Col. I see small villages begin,
Like twilight stars, to peep forth timidly,
Great distances apart; and now I see
Towns, swol'n to cities, burst upon the sight,
Thick as the crowded firmament at night.
I see brave science, with inspired soul,
Subdue the elements to its control;
On iron ways, through rock and mountain riven,

Impelling mighty freights, by vapor driven;
Or with electric nerves so interlace
The varied points of universal space.
Thought answers thought, though scores of miles between—
Time is outstripped——

King. We're not so jolly green.
My friend, come, ain't you getting rather steep?
We beg to probability you'll keep.
What see you now?

Col. The plethora of wealth
Corrupt and undermine the general health.
I see vile madd'ning fumes incite to strife,
Obscure the sense and whet the murderer's knife.
I see dead rabbits——

King. That's enough—give o'er;
It won't be prudent to see any more.
You've evidently over-taxed your head—
Just take a whiskey skin and go to bed.
Meantime, we give our royal approbation
To your grand scheme of general annexation,
And that in stealing gold you may not cease,
Receive the order of the "Golden Fleece."
I must keep dark—of course you have the "nous"
To pass judiciously the custom house.

Col. It will be hard, I know, to put the blinders
Upon the new marshall Don Isaiah Ryndors.
Our freight, mere farming implements we'll call—
A cargo of threshing machines—that's all.

King. The oyster trade just now is rather bad,
We know a couple of sloops that can be had
Dirt cheap for cash. We'll give you the command,
And you can start at once.

Col. I'll be on hand
At any moment, sire, that you propose—
My trunk is packed, when I put on my clothes.
Hope and your royal favor to my heart
Ambition impulse energy impart,
Ere long, like swelling sails, to be unfurled;
Blow, friendly gales, they'll bring you back a world.

King. Bring back a world! that would be, I must say,
Handsome return for such a small outlay.

Queen. Dear me! does anybody know how late
It is?

King. I don't for one.

Queen. It's half-past eight.

King. Good gracious!

Queen. Yes, indeed.

King. Well, don't you worry;
We'll go to bed, but as we're in a hurry—
The scene must operatically end—
We'll sing good night to our distinguished friend.

SLEEPY CHORUS, *with yawning accompaniment, in which it is hoped the spectators will not join.*

Fonseca. "Enchantress."

We are so nappy that to bed we must start,
The courtier doth easily lie;
To make us happy, though before we depart,
A night-cap I'll have on the sly.
Oh deary me, how sleepy are we,
Ye—ah!—aw! [*yawning,*] &c.

Duetto Cordiali. Ferdinand and Columbus.

Sonny, all right, good night,
We'll meet at breakfast in the morning,
And take a bite when the early light
Of the morn gets up, the dawn adorning.
In all the independent journals
We'll have a first-rate notice;
To succeed without the aid of the diurnals,
We know now-a-day no go 'tis, &c., &c.
[*All go off with bed candlesticks.*

SCENE II.—*A modest and retiring apartment in the palace.*

COLUMBUS *enters with a nightcap, which, in a moment of abstraction, he swallows.*

Col. I've made a precious bargain here, I swear—
This downey king expects the lion's share
And hasn't taken one, the common way
In which the poor world-worker gets his pay.
On one side, enterprise, toil, danger, death!
And on the other, mouthfuls of mere breath.
A vain man—worshipped, transitory name,
But ah! to sparkle in the heaven of fame
Eternal as itself, and life outlast,
Still ever-present in the living past.
To think one's memory may fill unsought
A Sovran throne within the realm of thought,
When piled up centuries their shadow flings
Across the records of forgotten kings;
What to such destiny are earthly joys?

FERDINAND, (*the king,*)—*in robe de chambre, and nightcapped —looks from door,* F.

King. Friend Christopher, you're making too much noise;
Please to remember this is not an inn.
Col I beg your pardon, sire, it was the gin;
By that, and your kind promises elated,
I own I did feel somewhat elevated.
King. Well, just blow off your froth and settle down. *Exit.*

Col. All right, your majesty. Oh, great renown,
What slights aspiring poverty endures
That through such patrons the great prize secures;
It riles me even now, to think this thing
In after ages to my fame will cling,
And like dead fruit upon the living tree,
Hang on to my green immortality.
Could this mean king, unless by my deserving,
Awake the genius of a Prescott or an Irving!
There's no use moralizing now, because
What will be will be, as what has been was.
And talking of what will be—a strange thought
Just crossed my mind with difficulty fraught:
If some small scribbler, in a future day,
Should try to weave my story in a play,
I'm curious now to know what he would do
For female interest to carry through
His plot, if any, for *my wife's* at home;
I couldn't ask her majesty to roam
Amongst my rude adventures—I guess
He'll find himself in a delightful mess.
He'll want a heroine, the rules despotic—
Hollo! that gin, by jingo, *is* narcotic. [*Yawns.*
Where can he find one? Out of some French play,
No doubt; that will be, then, the usual way.
French thought, French plot, French wit, French moral, cast,
And published, probably, by French, at last.
I'm going—going—gone. [*Sleeps.*

COLUMBIA *appears in luminous opening, at back—comes forward and touches* COLUMBUS, *who starts, and looks at her with astonishment.*

Colum. Columbus, wake!
Col. Hollo, ma'm, who are you, for gracious sake—
Attired in such extraordinary guise?
Colum. It's strange you should exhibit such surprise.
Don't you know your own child?
Col. I'm not so wise
A father.
Colum. No! nor yet old Uncle Sam?
Col. Haven't the honor.
Colum. Well, his niece I am,
In fact the genius of the mighty land
On which will rest your name and fame.
Col. I understand.
You're Hail Columbia, then—well, I declare,
I'm very glad to see you—take a chair.
Colum. Excuse me.
Col. From your cap and spangled bodice,
I took you first for Crawford's sculptured Goddess.
Colum And so I am—myself and Liberty
Are one

Col. Thus, undivided may you ever be.
Colum. I feel obliged.
Col. Pray tell me, if you please,
Are you that same liberty Demosthenes
So thundered for, until the cute invader
Beneath the patriot espied the trader,
And putting golden pebbles, it is said,
Into his mouth, shut up his noisy head?
Colum. Alas, I am, and *you* need not be told
That by such *patriots* I'm always sold.
Col. Likely enough; but may I make so bold
As most respectfully to ask, what is it
Produces me the honor of this visit?
Colum. Of course you know you're sleeping in that chair?
Col. I did *not* realize the fact, I swear.
But if you say that——
Colum. I assure you.
Col. Oh!
It's quite enough for you to tell me so.
Colum. You wish to know, then, why I made this call?
Col. If not too much to ask——
Colum. Oh, not at all.
You were just now much puzzled in your mind
In wondering where a dramatist could find
A heroine——
Col. Yes, I remember.
Colum. Look at me—
I mean, with you, to cross the Western Sea.
Col. But what induces you so far to roam?
Colum Simply the wish to reach my future home
As quickly as I can. By adverse fate
Compelled reluctantly to emigrate,
My business here is virtually ended,
The firm of "Freedom & Company" in fact suspended.
Col. I'm sorry to hear that—'twas my belief
That your investments here were just as safe
As—the Bank of England, I was going to say,
But lately that comparison won't pay.
Colum. But see, 'tis morning—your effects are stored,
The ship awaits us—shall we go on board?
Conveying Liberty, that humble bark
Unharmed shall ride, and like the primal ark,
Where its keel rests another world arise,
And Freedom hang its shingle on the skies.
Col. Are my prophetic visions, then, so near
Fulfilment? Oh, I feel uncommon queer;
Is it ambition so distracts my head,
Or last night's "tod" before I went to bed?
Colum Courage, Columbus; you have scenes of strife
Before you—even periling your life.

But I'll be with you in the hour of need.

Col. I'm very much obliged to you. indeed—
Thankful such guardianship to have secured.
Between ourselves *my* ship is not insured.

Colum. I'll take the risk. Behold our banner spread! [*Displays flag.*
Protection dwells within its folds.

Col. "Nuf ced."
I'm game to follow that, so go ahead.

SONG—*Columbus.* "*Star-Spangled Banner.*"

Oh, say, shall I see, ere my soul takes its flight,
Though the last ray of life should be fitfully gleaming,
A new country arise, on whose banner of light
Freedom's sons may behold the bright heaven of their dreaming.
Should a factious hand dare
Its proud folds to impair,
May it withering fall, and Columbia still bear
Her own star-spangled banner, forever to wave
O'er the land of the free and the home of the brave.
[*Exeunt,* L. H.

SCENE III.—*The stage represents the deck of the Santa Maria.*

COLUMBUS *and his rude assailers discovered in threatening atititudes.*

STRIKING CHORUS OF MUTINOUS MARINERS.

[*Taken from miscellaneous sources.*]

"Our captain swears he'll have his fling
So come let's fling him in the 'frigidum sine,'
For an old salt, 'tis just the thing,
At home he'll be in the middle of the briney."

Col. [*Sings.*] Must I be dished, while thus so surely
Verging on the land of Plato,
Its hard to be so prematurely
Dropped just like a hot potato.

Sancho. We'll give you one more chance unless you wish
To give a free lunch to the hungry fish,
You'd better take it, far enough we've come,
So just 'bout ship at once and let's go home.

Col. My home is on the rolling deep.

Pedro. In another minute
Your home, depend upon it, will be in it.

Bartol. We've made up our minds, our grub and grog
Are fading fast, there's not an egg for "nog"
Left in the hatchway, if you don't consent
To take the back track, it is our intent
To sack you first and then to sack your stores!

Col. Oh, men intractable, your chief implores
But one day longer!

Sancho. Not another hour!
All. No! no!
Col. Before such brutes 'tis cowardly to cower,
While I have life, right onward will I steer!
Bartol. We'll cut your tiller-ropes soon never fear!
No longer listen to his common pleas,
Seize the old tar and pitch him in the seas!
[*They make dangerous demonstrations.*
Col Oh! Spirit of my vision, where art thou?
On thee I call, redeem thy promise now!

Enter COLUMBIA.

Colum. She's here! [*Sailors shrink back in affright.*
Col. I'm saved!
Colum. What means this horrid din?
If its a free fight, you can count me in!
So many against one, now understand
To aid the weak I'll always be on hand!
Col. The Indian Empire's mine, your threats I mock
Rebellious *Sea*poys, now *I* "have-a-lock,"
Will shut you up!
Sancho. Hallo! My precious wig,
Here's a strange craft with a new fangled rig!
Where do you hail from?
Colum. Back, senseless crew!
'Tis just such mindless reprobates as you
That mar the calculations of the wise,
And clog the wheels of glorious enterprize!
Pedro. Pshaw! this palaver, mam's all very well,
But where we're driving to if you could tell,
We'd like it better.
Colum. [*To Columbus*] *You* are not so blind
But in the passing current you can find
Sure indications that the land is near.
Col. Within my heart I thought so, but the fear
Of raising hopes the end might not fulfil,
Stifled the new-born thought, and kept me still.
See! See! What's floating there?
Sancho. By jingo! greens!
And now I smell—
Pedro. What? Orange groves?
Sancho. No, pork and beans!
Pedro. Hogs! then hurrah! our tribulation ends,
Its very clear we're getting among friends!
Bartol. Look, look, here's something else now passing by.
[*They fish up a piece of Connecticut pastry.*
All. What is it?
Colum. What, you pumps, why pumpkin pie!
Sancho. What's this?
[*Fishes up immense walking-stick with knobs on it.*
A knobby stick

And on the knob
Inscribed distinctly—
All. What?
Sancho. "The Empire Club.
"The owner fitly will reward the finders
"If it's returned—"
All. To whom?
Sancho. "To Marshall Rynders.
[*A Play-Bill is fished up.*
All. What's this?
Colum. A bill of Burton's Theatre, you noodles!
Col. What are they doing now there?
Colum. "Sleek and Toodles."
Col. I hear the birds.
Colum. They're cat-birds if you do.
Col. The cat bird's song must be "the wild sea-mew,"
There's music somewhere nigh.
Colum. Don't be emphatic,
It's Dodworth's band on board the Adriatic,
She'll pass us soon upon her trial trip,
Look at her well, Columbus, such a ship
You never saw—and never will, I swow,
Unless he dream it, as he's doing now.
[*The Adriatic passes across, the Band playing "Yankee Doodle."*
Colum. See where she steams majestically down.
Sancho. My eyes and limbs, why it's a floating town!
Col. Right against wind and tide and not a sail,
The flying dutchman, that is, without fail:
Hurrah! look there, I'll take my oath I spy land!
Colum. Of course you do.
Col. What is it?
Colum. Coney Island!
[*All the sailors cluster around Columbus.*
Sancho. Oh, glorious admiral, upon our knees
We ask forgiveness—
Col. See what men are these
Attired in such extraordinary style?
Colum. They are the magnates of Manhatta's Isle,
Every distinguished guest they're bound to meet
And feed—don't fear, they can afford to treat,
For hospitality's a public trait,
Therefore the public can't object to pay.

[*Castle Garden extends itself from the Battery. Pier No.* 1 *appears, crowded with Reception Committees, &c. Columbus landed with the usual honors. "That Gun" takes its usual noisy part in the demonstration. Columbus is surrounded by enthusiastic admirers. Columbia remains unnoticed in the back-ground. Banners displayed on which are inscribed "Columbus for Mayor," "The People's Choice." "Columbus for Governor—Down with anybody else," "Columbus for President," "Liberty for ever," "Who dare oppose us."*

1st Cit. Welcome, old tar!
2d Cit. Old fellow, how do you do?
Col. Exceedingly well, I thank you, how are you?
1st Committee Man. Here, take my arm and let's escape the crowd.
2d C. M. Hello! this pipe-laying can't be allowed!
His party has no chance, sir, we can lick it,
With such a name as yours upon our ticket.
C. Man. You see we've lost no time. [*Points to Banners.*
Three cheers for Columbus! [*They cheer vociferously.*
Colum. As I expected
By those time servers, I'm of course neglected.
2d Com. Keep silence there for the address!
[*About to read long document*
1st Com. Go 'long!
Dry up! Where's Kerrigan? let's have a song!
All. Hurrah! a song, a song!

FINALE—*Dis-concerted piece, by the antagonistic Politicians.*

Chorus, " Gustave " Vive le Roi.

Swearing death to all who cave
What care we for the law?
He who bolts, we'll touch the knave
On the raw, on the raw.
Hearts that gold and rum inspire
Legal threats ne'er can fright,
He who slumps we'll knock him higher
Than a kite, than a kite.

Infernal Row, a la Robert le Diable.

Sound the tangrang and the hibang
Let the cowbell ding-dong;
Blow the riprack and the gripsack.
And the soft hotel gong!
Shout away it does'nt matter what you say,
Tol de dol de diddle day.

The Curtain Falls to Babylonish Confusion.

END OF ACT I.

ACT II.

SCENE I.—*In which the spectators are gratified by another view of the same palace, but in an empty state. It being the 1st of May* HIS MAJESTY *moves in, followed by* RODRIGUEZ DE FONSECA.

King. Archbishop, we're dyspeptic, dull, ennuyed,
And some amusement very sadly need.
Fon. Sire, I'm your soul's physician, solely, so,
What medicine to prescribe I hardly know,
The operatic folk are here to day,
And give, I'm told, a splendid *matinee.*
The sweetest singing birds I understand
That ever came from song's own native land,
Delicious Italy!
King. Delicious goose!
You know the squalling's only an excuse,
The whole affair you may depend upon its
Only an opening show of new spring bonnets.
Fon. A play perhaps might quicken your sensations.
King. I'm sick of local plays and French translations.
Fon. The model artistes—
King. [*Virtuously indignant*] What?
Fon. Not as orig*nally*
Shown, but etherialized---there's a new ballet.
King. No, no, I'm tired of their old Grandpas,
And can't translate their jumps and entrechats.
Fonseca. Some painting's have arrived, sir, which are said
To be superior.
King. Is the artist dead?
Fonseca. Not yet, my liege, I think.
King. Ah, that's a pity
They won't sell 'till he *is*, in this great city.
Fonseca. I scarce know what amusement to propose—
Were you in temper for exciting shows
We might go hear the aldermen debate,
Or the police commissioners dilate
On party straws, while through the city's walks
High-handed rowdyism rampant stalks.
King. Be good enough to change the conversation
We cannot help the city's situation,
If it's inhabitants don't watch the game
And see all's fair, they've but themselves to blame
Rule or mis-rule depends upon their voice
They pay's their money and they has their choice,
Can you suggest no kind of recreation
To quell this hypochandriac sensation?
Fonseca Well, let's see, Sire—if you have the leisure
You might, combining piety and pleasure,

Cook a few heretics.

King. [*Rising up.*] That *would* drive off the blues!
I *could* enjoy a dozen roasted Jews
On the half-shell—

Fonseca. Sire, I regret to say
We're out of Jews, upon your last birth day.
We dressed them all.

King. Why, what a burning shame!
Is there nothing unorthodox that you could name?

Fonseca. Scores of poor debtor's in our prison's dwell—

King. Would rather fry of course,—they'll do as well.

Enter DIEGO, *unceremoniously.*

King. What ho! Diego, whence this anxious face?

Diego. [*Present's Telegraph.*] A Telegraph, your highness, from Cape Race.

King. For us it seems—well, what of that, my lad?

Diego. Sire, I'm in hopes there may be news from dad!

King. [*Unfolding strip of paper.*
Faith it's extensive, from it's length I guess
T'was meant for the assoicated press! [*Reads.*
" Discount increased"—"Fund's easy"—" Cotton"—bother!
" The Queen's expected soon to have another"—

Diego and Fonseca. [*Naturally surprised.*] What?

King. " Drawing room"—Pshaw! they leave that line set up
" Improved stock"—" Agricultural prize cup"—
Ah! here we are—" Now coming through the sound
The Sloop Santa Maria homeward bound.
"Columbus master—from the Indian oceans,
" Freighted with odds and ends, and Yankee Notions."

Diego. Dad coming home! huzza! I hope and trust
The old boy's brought back plenty of the dust
If so his pockets will be soon attacked,
I'm deuced short just now, and that's a fact.

King. Our admiral returned, with lots of gold
Of course, our Bell this good news must be told!
Ah! here she is!

Enter ISABELLA *and the whole Court.*

King. Come, Bell, our oceanic stock's
Right up, we'll have a pocket full of rocks.

Queen. I'm glad to hear such welcome sounds as these!
Beck's bill is stiff and so is Tiffanny's.

Fonseca. Columbus back! from him I'll take the shine
Or else his star will overshadow mine.

King. We're in such jolly spirits we could sing—
And will—play up! [*To leader of orchestra.*

Leader. What, sire?

King. Oh! anything.

Leader. The gold song from " Robert?"

King. That's just the thing!

Singular vocal melange—KING.—" *Robert le Diable.*

Gold, gold, gold, is no chimera
Though sung to the opera stalls,
Bold, bold, bold, to risk so queer-a
Joke within the opera walls,
Where so much capital moulders
And the dividends don't come along
Every blessed shareholder's
Most unmistakably sold for a song.

Choral interruption—"*Rigoletto*"

Hard times, bard times, we've suffered
Enough by the hard times
Par-times, par-times, we'll soon have the regular par-times!
Star times, star times, Columbus will bring in the star times!
Let's meet him, and greet him
With a hip! hip! hip! hurrah!

Selfish and unprincipled solo—FONSECA.—" *Poor Soldier.*"

Now the money panic,
Lately so tyranic,
Is bound to start it's apple-cart
Before the " Oceanic."
Oh! the " Oceanic!"
I owe the " Oceanic"
A heap for shares, so unawares
Must " *bear*" the " Oceanic."

Solo—DIEGO—" *The Quaker's Wife.*"

Father and I are both in town,
For up he's got to poney,
Or I shall have to simmer down,
And think of matrimony.

Her Majesty signifies her intentions—"*Jeannette and Jeannot.*"

Oh! I'll have such brilliant parties now as never yet were seen,
For lately my allowance was particularly mean,
But now the specie's flowing in, the banks will all be flush,
And you had best believe it, that we'll go it with a rush.

"*Lucy Neal.*"

And all will you see kneel,
Oh, all will you see kneel,
Before the great and mighty dollar
All will *you* see kneel.

Enter FERNANDO.

Fernando. My liege! my liege!
King. Why, what irruption's this?
Or rather interruption, what's amiss?
Fernando. Nothing, my liege, I bear you welcome news!
Columbus!
King. That's another pair of shoes!
Has he returned?
Fernando. Just landed, and I'm told
Has brought you, sire, about a ton of gold!
King and all. A ton!
Fernando. More or less,
As New Year's gifts he brings
From the New World such rare and curious things
As he could pick up in so short a stay
Which at your royal feet he beg's to lay!
King. Now curiosity our bosom shakes!
We grant his suit, go hurry up the cakes!
Fonseca. Your highness, this ambitious man I fear,
Puffed by success, will cause disturbance here.
King. Don't be alarmed, we know what we're about;
When we have turned the vagrant inside out
In kingly style—away he'll have to pack—
We'll take his presents and give him the sack.
[*All the courtiers crowd the sides, kept back by guards.*
Fonseca. Where are you pushing to! stand back!

[*The Trans-Atlantic procession files in in the following order: A small detachment of Police to clear the way—a group of Indian slipper and smoking cap sellers, with their banner. A glass ballot box, carried by a politician of character, supported by a few distinguished members of the "Dead Rabbit Club." The Prince of Humbugs, mounted on a superbly-caparisoned woolly horse, and attended by a live mermaid and the nurse of Washington. Two Ethiopians, bearing respectively a mint julep and a sherry cobbler. Cuttle, Sleek and Toodles, arm-in-arm. King Powhattan, Pocahontas and John Smith. The Almighty Dollar, in regal robes, and promiscuously attended. All the States, represented by beautiful young ladies, surrounding* COLUMBUS. *An allegorical mask, interrupted by noise without.*

Col. What tumult's that?
New York. Miss Kansas, I suppose
She's crying to get in.
Col. What, with her bleeding nose?
I told her she would have to wait a cure,
And when her Constitution could endure
Fatigue, she might come in. Why here she is!

[KANSAS *enters and causes great confusion among the States, the* IMP OF DISCORD *attends her, who is finally quelled by* COLUMBIA, *and harmony is restored.*

King. Columbus, we are pleased.
Queen. And we—
King. Keep shady!
Bell. Won't you introduce me to your lady? [*To* Col.
Col. Only too proud. Columbia!
Colum. I'm on hand!
Col. Let me present you to King Ferdinand,
Queen Isabella.

[Columbia *shakes hand energetically with their majesties to the great consternation of the Court.*

Colum. Hollo! What's out?
Col. My pet,
You've outraged all the rules of ettiquette.
Colum. What should I do?
Fon. Why kneel, the rules demand it.
Colum. I can't—my constitution wouldn't stand it.
King. We'll wave the ceremonial. Can these be
Your children that we look at?
Colum. Yes, sirree!
I have a few more young uns on the "farms"
Besides one most unruly babe in "arms,"
Miss Utah, but we soon shall cure her ills
With some steel drops and "*Harney's*" leaden-pills!
King. Columbus, what reward can we bestow
On you for giving us this goodly show?
Col. My liege if I've accomplished well my task
And gained your favor, it is all I ask.
Our fillibustering scheme I've carried through,
The country's safe, and now belongs to you.
Bye and bye, perhaps, when they've experience bought,
They may return us the same blow we taught.
King. Such magnanimity our bosom charms,
So we present you with—a coat of arms,
Together with the name and rank of "Don—"
Fon. My liege, our precincts now you trench upon,
'Twill be bad precedent to lift poor merit
Up to their level, who by blood inherit.
What has he done except what I or you
Or any accidental fool could do?
Colum. I'll tell you—
Col. Don't be riled, I'll see you through,
Bring me an egg. [*The egg is brought.*
If you're with skill endowed
To make this egg stand up, I'll treat the crowd.
[*They individually try the experiment which is a failure all round.*
Diego. I'm beat!
Fernando. I'm sold!
King. We're bothered.
Fon. Where's the fun

In this? It's evident it can't be done.
Colum. Oh! yes it can!
King. We'd like to see the way.
Fon. I'll stake my head it can't!
Colum. "A dreadful lay,"
Here's to decide it! Now behold, oh king,
What great effects from such slight cause will spring!

[*Gong. The scene shifts for itself and discovers the egg of Columbus, being much magnified, which changes to the Temple of Fame, in which are grouped a selection from American celebrities on a pyramid. Columbus takes his place.*

Finale.—"Hail Columbia."

Hail Columbia's honored band,
Hail ye worthies of the land,
By freedom broke
From the foreign yoke,
We the benignant stars invoke
Protection evermore,
To shed upon thy friendly shore.
May Columbia's happy land,
Rifted by no traitor hand
United be
From sea to sea
The home of *Peace* and *Liberty!*

THE END.

[*Catalogue continued from second page of cover.*]

VOL. XXV.	VOL. XXVI.
193 Father and Son,	201 Adrienne the Actress
194 Massaniello,	202 Undine,
195 Sixteen String Jack,	
196 Youthful Queen,	
197 Skeleton Witness,	
198 Inkeep'r of Abbeville	
199 Miller and his Men,	
200 Aladdin.	

HAMLET, in Three Acts, condensed and adapted by WALTER GAY. Price, 12½ cts.

THE SPANISH WIFE; by SAMUEL M. SMUCKER, Esq., with a Portrait and Memoir of EDWIN FORREST. Price 12½ cents.

THE OATH OF OFFICE; by CHARLES JAMES CANNON, Esq., with a Portrait of the Author. Price 12½ cents.

GUTTLE AND GULPIT. Price 12½ cents.

Plays 12½ Cents Each. Bound Volumes, $1.

☞ Plays sent by mail, and postage pre-paid, on receipt of 12½ cents each, in money or stamps. Ten plays sent by express for one dollar.

PLAYS IN FRENCH AND ENGLISH.

THE ORIGINAL FRENCH COPY,

WITH A LITERAL ENGLISH TRANSLATION,

ADAPTED FOR SCHOOLS AND PRIVATE READING.

VOLUME I.

ANGELO; or, the Tyrant of Padua. A Drama in 3 Acts....By VICTOR HUGO
LADY TARTUFFE. Prose Comedy in 5 Acts....By MME. EMILE DE GIRARDIN
ANDROMACHE. A Tragedy in 5 Acts....By RACINE
THE RIGHT LINE. A Comedy in 1 Act....By MARC MONNIER
PHÆDRA. A Tragedy in 5 Acts....By RACINE
HORACE AND LYDIA. A Comedy in 1 Act....By F. PONSARD
SPARROW OF LYSBIA. A Comedy in 1 Act....By ARMAUD BARTHET

VOLUME II.

HORATIUS. A Tragedy in 4 Acts....By CORNEILLE
VIRGINIA. A Tragedy in 5 Acts....By M. LATOUR
MARY STUART. A Tragedy in 5 Acts....By M. PIERRE LEBRUN
M'LLE DE BELLE ISLE. A Drama in 5 Acts....By ALEXANDRE DUMAS
POLYEUCTES THE MARTYR. A Christain Tragedy....By CORNEILLE
ADRIENNE LECOUVREUR. A Drama in 5 Acts....By M. M. SCRIBE and LEGOVE

☞ The above, which were originally published at 25 and 50 cents, for single Plays, are now reduced to less than half price.

*** PRICE FOR THE VOLUMES—Handsomely Bound, with Flexible Covers, $1 each. Single Plays, 15 cents each.—eight for $1.

☞ Sent by mail, post-paid, on receipt of Price.

MASSEY'S EXHIBITION RECITER,

AND

DRAWING ROOM ENTERTAINMENTS,

Being choice Recitations in Prose and Verse. Together with an unique Collection of Petite Comedies, Dramas and Farces—adapted for the use of Schools and Families.

BY CHARLES MASSEY,

Professor of Elocution at Burlington College, N. J., and Mechanics' Society School, New York.

No 1 CONTAINS

Guy Fawkes; An Historical Drama.
The Man with the Carpet Bag; A Farce.
White Horse of the Peppers; A Comic Drama.
Mesmerism; A Petite Comedy.
And Twelve selected Pieces.

No. 2 CONTAINS

Love and Jealousy; A Tragedy.
The Irish Tutor; A Farce.
Bombastes Furioso: A Burlesque Opera
Sylvester Daggerwood; Comic Interlude.
School for Orators; An Original Comedy
And Eighteen Selected Pieces.

☞ Price per Number, Paper Covers, 25 cts. each. The two Numbers bound in Cloth, School Style, 60 cents.

☞ Sent by mail, post-paid, on receipt of Price.

☞ All orders will receive prompt attention. ☞ A New Play will be published every week.

S. FRENCH, 122 NASSAU STREET, (up stairs,) N. Y.

☞ Important change in the postage law: All transient matter must be pre-paid.

FRENCH'S MINOR DRAMA.

Price 12½ Cents each.—Bound Volumes $1.

VOL. I.

1 The Irish Attorney,
2 Boots at the Swan,
3 How to Pay the Rent,
4 The Loan of a Lover,
5 The Dead Shot,
6 His Last Legs,
7 The Invisible Prince,
8 The Golden Farmer.

With a Portrait and Memoir of JOHN SEFTON.

VOL. II.

9. Pride of the Market,
10. Used Up,
11. The Irish Tutor,
12. The Barrack Room,
13. Luke the Laborer,
14. Beauty and the Beast,
15. St. Patrick's Eve,
16. Captain of the Watch.

With a Portrait and Memoir of Miss C. WEMYSS.

VOL. III.

17 The Secret, [Peppers
18 White Horse of the
19 The Jacobite,
20 The Bottle.
21 Box and Cox,
22 Bamboozling,
23 Widow's Victim,
24 Robert Macaire.

With a Portrait and Memoir of Mr. F. S. CHANFRAU.

VOL. IV.

25 Secret Service,
26 Omnibus,
27. Irish Lion,
28. Maid of Croissy,
29. The Old Guard,
30. Raising the Wind,
31. Slasher and Crasher,
32. Naval Engagements.

With a Portrait and Memoir of Miss ROSE TELBIN.

VOL. V.

33. Cocknies in California
34. Who Speaks First?
35. Bombastes Furioso,
36. Macbeth Travestie.
37. Irish Ambassador,
38. Delicate Ground,
39. The Weathercock,
40. All that Glitters is not Gold.

With a Portrait and Memoir of W. A. GOOALL.

VOL. VI.

41. Grimshaw, Bagshaw and Bradshaw,
42. Rough Diamond,
43. Bloomer Costume,
44. Two Bonnycastles,
45. Born to Good Luck,
46. Kiss in the Dark,
47. 'Twould Puzzle a Conjuror,
48. Kill or Cure.

With a Portrait and Memoir of F. M. KENT.

VOL. VII.

49 Box and Cox Married
50 St. Cupid [and Settled
51 Go-to-bed Tom,
52 The Lawyers,
53 Jack Sheppard,
54 The Toodles,
55 The Mobcap,
56 Ladies Beware.

With a Portrait and Memoir of SOL. SMITH.

VOL. VIII.

57 Morning Call,
58 Popping the Question,
59 Deaf as a Post,
60 New Footman,
61 Pleasant Neighbor,
62 Paddy the Piper,
63 Brian O'Linn,
64 Irish Assurance.

VOL. IX.

65 Temptation.
66 Paddy Carey,
67 Two Gregories,
68 King Charming,
69 Po-ca-hon-tas,
70 Clockmaker's Hat,
71 Married Rake,
72 Love and Murder.

VOL. X.

73 Ireland and America,
74 Pretty Piece of Business,
75 Irish Broom-maker,
76 To Paris and Back for Five Pounds,
77 That Blessed Baby,
78 Our Gal,
79 Swiss Cottage,
80 Young Widow.

VOL. XI.

81 O'Flannigan and the
82 Irish Post, [Faries
83 My Neighbor's Wife,
84 Irish Tiger,
85 P.P., or Man & Tiger,
86 To Oblige Benson,
87 State Secrets,
88 Irish Yankee.

VOL. XII.

89 A Good Fellow,
90 Cherry and Fair Star,
91 Gale Breezely,
92 Our Jemimy,
93 Miller's Maid,
94 Awkward Arrival,
95 Crossing the Line,
96 Conjugal Lesson.

VOL. XIII.

97 My Wife's Mirror,
98 Life in New York,
99 Middy Ashore,
100 Crown Prince,
101 Two Queens,
102 Thumping Legacy,
103 Unfinished Gentleman
104 House Dog.

VOL. XIV.

105 The Demon Lover,
106 Matrimony,
107 In and Out of Place,
108 I Dine with My Mo-
109 Hi-a-wa-tha, [ther,
110 Andy Blake,
111 Love in '76, [culties
112 Romance under Diffi-

VOL. XV.

113 One Coat for 2 Suits,
114 A Decided Case,
115 Daughter, [Minority,
116 No; or, the Glorious
117 Coroner's Inquisition
118 Love in Humble Life,
119 Family Jars,
120 Personation.

VOL. XVI.

121 Children in the Wood
122 Winning a Husband,
123 Day after the Fair,
124 Make Your Wills,
125 Rendezvous,
126 My Wife's Husband,
127 Monsieur Tonson,
128 Illustrious Stranger.

VOL. XVII.

129 Mischief-Making,
130 A Live Woman in the
131 The Corsair, [Mines,
132 Shylock,
133 Spoiled Child,
134 Evil Eye,
135 Nothing to Nurse,
136 Wanted a Widow.

VOL. XVIII.

137 Lottery Ticket,
138 Fortune's Frolic,
139 Is he Jealous?
140 Married Bachelor,
141 Husband at Sight,
142 Irishman in London,
143 Animal Magnetism,
144 Highways & By-Ways

VOL. XIX.

145 Columbus, [Beard,
146 Harlequin Blue

PLAYS 12½ CENTS EACH—BOUND VOLUMES, $1.

☞ Plays sent by mail, and postage paid, on receipt of 12½ cents each, in money or stamps. Ten Plays sent by Express for one dollar.

*** All orders will receive prompt attention. A new Play published every week.

☞ An Alphabetical List of 850 Plays sent by mail on receipt of a postage stamp.

SAMUEL FRENCH, Publisher,
122 NASSAU ST., (up stairs.)

☞ See List of Standard Drama on second and third pages of Cover.

www.ingramcontent.com/pod-product-compliance
Lightning Source LLC
LaVergne TN
LVHW011138110826
845150LV00008B/2392

* 9 7 8 1 4 1 8 1 9 3 1 6 4 *